MW00915116

*GREATER
ALSO AVAILABLE IN EBOOK AND
AUDIOBOOK FORMAT.

Greater Than a Tourist Book Series Reviews from Readers

I think the series is wonderful and beneficial for tourists to get information before visiting the city.

-Seckin Zumbul, Izmir Turkey

I am a world traveler who has read many trip guides but this one really made a difference for me. I would call it a heartfelt creation of a local guide expert instead of just a guide.

-Susy, Isla Holbox, Mexico

New to the area like me, this is a must have!

-Joe, Bloomington, USA

This is a good series that gets down to it when looking for things to do at your destination without having to read a novel for just a few ideas.

-Rachel, Monterey, USA

Good information to have to plan my trip to this destination.

-Pennie Farrell, Mexico

Great ideas for a port day.

-Mary Martin USA

Aptly titled, you won't just be a tourist after reading this book. You'll be greater than a tourist!

-Alan Warner, Grand Rapids, USA

Even though I only have three days to spend in San Miguel in an upcoming visit, I will use the author's suggestions to guide some of my time there. An easy read - with chapters named to guide me in directions I want to go.

-Robert Catapano, USA

Great insights from a local perspective! Useful information and a very good value!

-Sarah, USA

This series provides an in-depth experience through the eyes of a local. Reading these series will help you to travel the city in with confidence and it'll make your journey a unique one.

-Andrew Teoh, Ipoh, Malaysia

GREATER THAN A TOURIST-PALM SPRINGS CALIFORNIA USA

50 Travel Tips from a Local

Joan Schneider

The statements in this book are of the authors and may not be the views of
CZYK Publishing or Greater Than a Tourist.
First Edition
Cover designed by: Ivana Stamenkovic
Cover Image: https://pixabay.com/photos/palm-springs-california-palm-trees-
1587288/

Image 1: By Patrick Nouhailler - Palm Springs is a desert city in Riverside County,
California, within the Coachella Valley - USA - January 2010 - Patrick Nouhailler, CC BY-
SA 2.0, https://commons.wikimedia.org/w/index.php?curid=116724625
Image 2: By Visitor7 - Own work, CC BY-SA 3.0,
https://commons.wikimedia.org/w/index.php?curid=26341337
Image 3: By Sidvics - Own work, CC BY-SA 3.0,
https://commons.wikimedia.org/w/index.php?curid=40294667
Image 4: By Carol M. Highsmith - Library of CongressCatalog:
http://lccn.loc.gov/2013631304Image download:
https://cdn.loc.gov/master/pnp/highsm/24100/24126a.tifOriginal url:
http://hdl.loc.gov/loc.pnp/highsm.24126, Public Domain,
https://commons.wikimedia.org/w/index.php?curid=51056729

CZYK Publishing Since 2011.
CZYKPublishing.com
Greater Than a Tourist
Lock Haven, PA
All rights reserved.
ISBN: 9798826086407

>TOURIST

50 TRAVEL TIPS FROM A LOCAL

BOOK DESCRIPTION

With travel tips and culture in our guidebooks written by a local, it is never too late to visit Palm Springs. Greater Than a Tourist- Palm Springs, California, USA by Joan Schneider offers the inside scoop on historic Palm Springs. Most travel books tell you how to travel like a tourist. Although there is nothing wrong with that, as part of the 'Greater Than a Tourist' series, this book will give you candid travel tips from someone who has lived at your next travel destination. This guide book will not tell you exact addresses or store hours but instead gives you knowledge that you may not find in other smaller print travel books. Experience cultural, culinary delights, and attractions with the guidance of a Local. Slow down and get to know the people with this invaluable guide. By the time you finish this book, you will be eager and prepared to discover new activities at your next travel destination.

Inside this travel guide book you will find:

Visitor information from a Local
Tour ideas and inspiration
Valuable guidebook information

Greater Than a Tourist- A Travel Guidebook with 50 Travel Tips from a Local. Slow down, stay in one place, and get to know the people and culture. By the time you finish this book, you will be eager and prepared to travel to your next destination.

OUR STORY

Traveling is a passion of the Greater than a Tourist book series creator. Lisa studied abroad in college, and for their honeymoon Lisa and her husband toured Europe. During her travels to Malta, an older man tried to give her some advice based on his own experience living on the island since he was a young boy. She was not sure if she should talk to the stranger but was interested in his advice. When traveling to some places she was wary to talk to locals because she was afraid that they weren't being genuine. Through her travels, Lisa learned how much locals had to share with tourists. Lisa created the Greater Than a Tourist book series to help connect people with locals. A topic that locals are very passionate about sharing.

TABLE OF CONTENTS

DEDICATION

This book is dedicated to Abe who took a chance and moved under the desert wind and starry sky.

ABOUT THE AUTHOR

Joan is an LA native who lives in Palm Springs and is an avid cyclist, writer, and affiliate marketer. Joan loves to visit desolate desert communities and dance under the night sky. She prefers to write in the back row of eclectic cafes and on airplanes, always on the right side.

Joan also loves to travel…

HOW TO USE THIS BOOK

The *Greater Than a Tourist* book series was written by someone who has lived in an area for over three months. The goal of this book is to help travelers either dream or experience different locations by providing opinions from a local. The author has made suggestions based on their own experiences. Please check before traveling to the area in case the suggested places are unavailable.

Travel Advisories: As a first step in planning any trip abroad, check the Travel Advisories for your intended destination.
https://travel.state.gov/content/travel/en/
traveladvisories/traveladvisories.html

FROM THE PUBLISHER

Traveling can be one of the most important parts of a person's life. The anticipation and memories that you have are some of the best. As a publisher of the Greater Than a Tourist, as well as the popular *50 Things to Know* book series, we strive to help you learn about new places, spark your imagination, and inspire you. Wherever you are and whatever you do I wish you safe, fun, and inspiring travel.

Lisa Rusczyk Ed. D.
CZYK Publishing

WELCOME TO
> TOURIST

Palm Springs is a desert city in Riverside County, California, within the Coachella Valley

A wind farm in Palm Springs, California, north of the Museum Trail

Palm Springs - Tahquitz Canyon Way - Agosto 2011

The Hotel California, a boutique hotel in Palm Springs, California

*"Once a year, go somewhere
you have never been before"*

- Dalai Lama.

Palm Springs is not just a town where people rent out midcentury modern homes with sparkling pools and celebrate their Bachelorette party. Since my years of living in Palm Springs, I developed a passion for historic Spanish style architecture and desert wildlife. I hope to share some of that love with you as a local's view of the areas of Palm Springs not widely known.

1. FOREVER MARILYN

While searching for vacation rentals, one would likely find artwork of the famous Marilyn Monroe plastered in bedroom walls. The history runs deep. In 1949, at the age of 22, Marilyn was discovered at one of the famous racquet clubs. Since her discovery she has been one of the most iconic names in Hollywood due to her aesthetic appeal and her charisma. As of 2022, the 10-year-old 26 ft tall statue of Marilyn now lives in front of the Palm Springs art museum, facing

Palm Canyon Drive which is the most popular tourist spot. There's nothing that screams Palm Springs like taking a selfie with a giant Marilyn sculpture.

2. PALM SPRINGS HIKES

A good amount of land in Palm Springs is owned by the Indian tribe, Agua Caliente Band of Cahuilla Indians. For that reason, a lot of the most popular hikes, Indian Canyons and Tahquitz Canyon charge a fee for people to hike on their land. Tahquitz is a 1.90 miles loop and has a sensational 60-foot waterwall. The spring fed waters start high above the ground and cascade down the mountain forming this clear pool where bighorn sheep like to drink from. Indian Canyons is a 1-mile loop, home to more than 150 species of plants that surround a lush palm oasis that brings shade on a warm day of hiking. Both hikes will cost anywhere from $12- $15 per person, per hike. Winter and early spring are best times for these hikes before the spike in heat.

3. CAN'T HAVE ENOUGH LINEN

Linen is the fabric of Palm Springs. Since Palm Springs in the summer can reach temperatures of over 120 degrees, it's essential to be prepared. Light linen is the best to keep your body cool while exploring in the heat. Palm Springs is over 100 degrees for 3-4 months of the year so if you are visiting in those summer months, weather preparedness is essential. Linen paired with a light-colored hat is the best defense. Bonus points for bringing an umbrella and using it as a "sunbrella". Be prepared to apply sunscreen every couple of hours and take breaks from being in the sun. The desert sun is not forgiving.

4. DRIVE SLOW

Palm Springs is known for being a resort town. The city is filled with tourists who go to catch up on some rest and relaxation by the poolside. Driving down Palm Canyon, you'll be welcomed by the San Jacinto mountains in the west, San Bernadino mountains in the west, and the Santa Rosa mountains in the South. During your stay you'll likely see some classic cars from the 50's and 60's driving slow along the road. If you have time, go to the shops for a test drive.

5. MAKE RESERVATIONS IN ADVANCE

With many new restaurants, a mix of new and old, you must make sure to book tables in advance. The most iconic historic restaurants such as Melvyn's and Spencer's are normally booked up for day-of reservations. The best thing to do is to book an early reservation pre 6pm and walk around downtown after.

6. BUDDING WITH MOVIE STARS

In the 1930's movie stars flocked to Palm Springs as a place to get out of the limelight and to catch some rays. Bob Hope, Frank Sinatra, and Dean Martin were a few of the pioneers who bought second homes in Palm Springs. Some celebrities enjoyed Palm Springs so much that they opened iconic racquet clubs and private communities that would house the most wealthy and powerful folks of the era. The Hollywood appeal still pulses through the veins of the town.

7. T-33 THUNDERBIRD

Ever want to ride in a historic WWII war plane? At the Palm Springs air museum you can take a 30min flight on numerous planes ranging from the P-51D Mustang, a premier fighter aircraft to the T-6 Texan, an advanced training aircraft during WWII for US fighter pilots. Visit the museum and stay for the tours. You must book in advance to ensure availability. The air museum always gets packed on weekends when history buffs flock in.

8. CACTUS ENVY

Cacti are a part of the plantae kingdom and are part of the cactaceae family. There are ties to about 1750 other known species, all similar in look and feel. However, some are vastly unique. Palm Springs has their own botanical garden specializing in the cacti family. There are thousands of specimens located in a one acre garden that is categorized geographically. Visit Morteen, Palm Springs iconic cactus garden and take a stroll to learn about the cacti around the world from Baja to South Africa. Guided tours are also available and there's an opportunity to take home your very own slice of cacti heaven. Admission costs $5-10 depending on the day and time.

9. HISTORIC BARN VIBES

Palm Springs is known for their mid century modern, alexander homes. Amidst the rows of single level flat roofs and exposed neutral colored brick lies Sparrow's Lodge. Sparrow's was one of the original getaways to host Hollywood Elite. The restored 1950's rustic 20 room boutique hotel that is fitted with wood beams, red walls, and concrete floors. There are no televisions in the rooms, and you sleep to the sound of the waterfall outside your private exterior living space. How's that for solace? Sparrows features a farm to table restaurant embellished with outdoor lights that light up the sky for evening dining.

This is a great place to get away from the hustle and bustle.

During the summer when hotel prices drop, you can get this stay for 1/3 of the typical nightly fee. This is for those who do not mind being in 110+ pool weather. The pool will be cooled, and waitresses and waiters are highly attentive to serve drinks and snacks by the cabana chaises.

10. RICH FLAVORS OF MEXICO

Eclectic mariachi music welcomes you in as you grab a 1980's barrel chair at the table. The homemade chips and salsa come to your table less than a minute from sitting down. The servers ask, "The usual? Burrito pequeno, pozole, taco plate, and a bohemia?" With so many Mexican restaurants in Palm Springs, Taqueria Tlaquepaque has made a name for itself due to its homage to traditional Mexican food. The prices are reasonable while other Mexican restaurants that outline downtown are charge double. Tlaquepaque recently upgraded their location to Palm Canyon in the last year since they needed more space to expand. That's when you know, the food is solid.

For those who are searching for a place to throw a casual event, this is the place. They have a private room fitted with TV's and has seating for ~25+. This would be the perfect spot to throw graduation parties, Cinco de mayo parties, or any other birthday parties.

11. MOVE OVER HOLLYWOOD, SEE THE STARS IN PALM SPRINGS

While walking down Palm Canyon Drive, you'll notice stars line the sidewalk, similar to those in Hollywood. The main difference is that these stars showcase local community heroes- humanitarians, architects, artists who have lived in Palm Springs sometime in their life. Elizabeth Taylor, Marilyn Monroe, and Truman Capote are on the list of stars embedded in the sidewalk pavement. Enjoy walking around downtown and see the stars below. If you stroll in the evening, look up and see a sky full of stars.

12. CALLING ALL ANIMAL LOVERS

If you are looking for a dog to adopt, or just want to learn about the local shelter and animal charities, stop by the Palm Springs animal shelter. Not only is the building a mid-century modern architectural masterpiece, but it's also, home to over 80 cats/dogs/guinea pigs who need happy homes. There's always an influx of new animals, so each time you visit you'll see a diverse crowd.

One of the many reasons why I love this place is that the folks working there are mostly volunteers. They are all intensely passionate about re-homing their animals and will do thorough due diligence to ensure dogs will be going to the right home. Be aware that dog or cat babies will be swooped up quickly. Monitor their website and make sure you can go day of to get the dog of your dreams. From time-to-time folks will visit the shelter hours before opening to ensure they are first in line to adopt the dog of their dreams.

The animal shelter is an important part of the Palm Springs community. They also throw fundraiser gala events which attract hundreds of folks to enjoy a night of dinner and dancing. There are numerous shops/restaurants that partner with the animal shelter to send them donations.

13. GIRAFFE FEEDING

Giraffes have particularly long tongues which allows them to reach even the highest, most hard to get leaves. See them up close and personal at the giraffe feeding which is daily at 9-3pm. The Living Desert Zoo is home to over 500 animals representing over 150 species. Walking around the grounds, you will see a lot of animals originally come from desert habitats. Some favorites are the desert bighorn sheep, rhinos, dromedary camel, striped hyena, and even a warthog.

If you plan to go in the summer, go as early as you can to escape the heat. Bring lots of water and take frequent heat breaks. For those who are big zoo fans, you may want to plan your trip around the summer months since weather can be unforgiving.

14. SWING LIKE THE PROS

Palm Springs is known for being a world class golf destination with world class weather year-round. Some popular golf ranges are the Tahquitz creek golf resort, Escena golf club, and Indian Canyons golf resort. These are all in Palm Springs proper. There are a ton more golf resorts in neighboring cities such as Rancho Mirage and Indian Wells. Many locals spend their days swinging at the holes, sipping on margaritas, and showing off their golf carts. With so much natural beauty, Palm Springs deserves the title as being one of the golf capitals of the world.

15. SPORT OF PALM SPRINGS

When you think of pickleball, think of a sport that has combined elements of tennis and ping pong, but using wiffle ball. You can play with 2 or 4 players. While you don't need to run a full tennis court to play, it's still an active sport. Demuth park is one of the few parks in Palm Springs that has pickleball courts. For that reason, they are also busy. Locals and tourists will come experience the iconic Palm Springs pickleball scene. People wait for hours to grab courts.

For those new to pickleball, you can take classes. There are classes to sign up for at the courts. The group sizes are small, and the classes have the option to meet once or twice a week. This is also a great way to meet others if you are visiting for an extended time.

16. PALM SPRINGS HISTORICAL SOCIETY

When walking down Palm Canyon Drive, do take a moment and stop at the Palm Springs historical society. The nonprofit organization was established in 1955 and it encompasses two of the oldest buildings in Palm Springs- McCallum Adobe and the Cornelia White House. Both houses are museums open for the public. Admission is free. The organization also hosts walking and biking tours that take place daily. Tour golden era Hollywood homes, Frank Sinatra's neighborhood, and see first glimpse into modernist homes from the 20's. Make reservations at least 24 hours in advance.

This is an organization living solely through volunteers. The staff are passionate about sharing the Palm Springs history with others. For those who might have some time to kill, visit the historical society and learn about the developments in the city that makes it what it's known for today.

17. PICNIC AT RUTH HARDY

If you are coming to visit Palm Springs in the winter or the early spring and the weather isn't yet 100 degrees, the best place for a picnic is at Ruth Hardy. This park is famously known as being one of the most appealing parks in the city due to it's vast 22 acres and immaculate sprawling green grass. The park also has 8 public tennis courts, 3 sand volleyball courts, picnic tables, and basketball courts. This a great place to bring your significant other or bring the family and pack the dogs!

On weekends, there are always events happening in the park. My favorite event I spotted before was a group of folks training their show dogs to jump through hoops and run through obstacles. Each dog had on a vibrant outfit, and some even had dyed hair. The owners had matching orange shirts with a highlighted yellow fringe. I suspect this was a monthly get together. You never know what you'll see when you pass by Ruth Hardy.

18. NOW THAT'S A REAL DELI

While at the park, don't forget your sandwiches. The best deli in town is the Real Italian Deli. Yes, the restaurant does live up to its name. You will find a taste of Italy in the middle of the desert. The menu often changes, but arguably the best sandwich is the turkey pesto. The baguette and pesto are made fresh in the morning. The baguette is so soft that you don't need to bite hard to tear the bread apart. The bread simply dissolves in your mouth. You cannot go wrong with this place. Have a large group? Pick up these sandwiches and expect compliments on the choice.

The deli has two locations, one in Palm Springs and one in Palm Desert. The Palm Desert location was the original and that one is fitted with many various Italian produce ready for folks to take home. You can find Dolce and Gabbana pasta and an assortment of unique noodles.

19. BABY ENVY

While many things in 2020 were bizarre, the bizarre doesn't quite stop there. Right outside the Palm Springs Museum, you'll notice these 11 feet long, 9 feet high statues of crawling babies. These were originally showcased in Prague, and the designer David Cerny has chosen Palm Springs as their next site. You've got to see them for yourself. This is another Palm Springs art staple.

20. VINTAGE AND ANTIQUE LOVERS

The neighborhood of Warm Sands has numerous vintage and antique stores that will keep you entertained for the entire day. One, the Antique Galleries of Palm Springs is fitted with dozens of antique vendors and display their art/ furniture/ goods in a 2-story building. There are so many antiques that the amount displayed at the shop could likely fill 10 stories. You could be in there for days on end. There are one of a kind 1980's Argentinean barrel chairs, 1930's mid century modern Scandinavian acacia wood tables, and original art from local artists. Sometimes you'll find the artists roaming around the grounds and you might catch yourself in an hour conversation around how the history of each piece in their collection. Make sure you have enough time to see everything. Prices are semi-negotiable. Artists make a living through the sale of these pieces, so don't low-ball offers. They will be politely refused.

For those war buffs, there's a room dedicated solely to history and artifacts from those time periods. I have an inkling towards the history of Titanic and was able to find a one-of-a-kind Titanic blueprint there which is now displayed with a black frame in my bathroom. The blueprint was reasonably priced and was in excellent condition as with many of the other artifacts in the building. The folks who work there are also history buffs so if you have a certain decade, or a certain object that you lust, they can help you find it fast. The shop is a well-oiled machine from the perspective of organization.

21. FEELING LUCKY?

Two streets off Palm Canyon Drive lies the Agua Caliente casino, where you'll find gaming, blackjack, poker, slots, and numerous table games. There's also a well-known steakhouse located inside the casino and is named one of best steakhouses in 2021 according to Forbes travel guide. Have a craft cocktail at the center bar and test your luck at the tables. Be aware, this is the spot to be for bachelorette parties. You may run into a couple different groups of brightly colored dresses rocking face paint. They normally don't bite.

There are multiple Agua Caliente casinos in the Coachella Valley. You'll find one in all the main cities including Palm Springs, which embraces the Palm Springs laid back vibe, Rancho Mirage which sets the standard for luxury, and Cathedral city, which is the newest property. Rancho mirage has an outdoor pool and is fitted with a five-star spa. Smoking is permitted at all locations.

22. THE INFAMOUS PUPU PLATTER

There's only one place you can get the Pupu in Palm Springs and that's at the Tropicale restaurant. The pupu is an exotic combination of chicken satay, beef skewers, coconut tiger shrimp, spring rolls, and ribs. Pair this with a house cabernet and call it a date night. Tropicale at night is known for being one of the liveliest restaurants in Palm Springs.

You are first welcomed by the neon lit sign in the entrance, then, you step in and see the dimly lit restaurant accentuated with live music and free flowing cocktails. The bar is totally full of folks waiting to get seats on the sides. Laughter and storytelling fill the air of the restaurant. Waiters and waitresses run back and forth handling plates topped with chicken skewers, steak and frites, and old fashion glasses. Book in advance to reserve your seat, it gets packed quickly no matter what day of the week.

23. PRIME ESTATE SALES

Palm Springs is home to many upscale estate sales where you'd be pleasantly surprised to find artifacts from the 1800, vintage Marc Chagall artwork, and Turkish wool rugs, to name a few. Some are a hit or miss, but the majority have something to offer. Check out the site: estatesales.net. If you're a vintage lover, or collector, there's something for you.

Always bring cash to the estate sales because most will not accept card. Also, you can view pictures of the sale online. If the pictures are attractive, go early. If the estate sale is marketed to start at 9am, go at 8:30 and be ready to wait in a line to be the first of those to view the sale. This is a very popular pastime for Palm Springs locals so be ready and go early.

24. SUSHI IN THE DESERT

Many people would turn their backs to the phenomenon of good sushi in the desert. I would agree, until I found this place, Taka Shin on Palm Canyon Drive. Taka Shin is a high-end sushi restaurant bringing in elegance and culinary art to the desert. Fish is seasonal. This restaurant is known for their omakase style dinners where you put your trust in the sushi chef and they create a custom dinner, tailored to your preferences based on availability, taste, and seasonality. Typically, these meals range anywhere from 5-10 dishes.

The best items on the menu are the spicy tuna roll, king salmon roll, otoro roll, mushroom soup, crispy rice, and Chilean sea bass miso yaki. The best tip is to sit at the sushi bar and watch the sushi chefs' work. Everything is prepared with the utmost of care and precision. The chefs' times each plate perfectly and artfully. They are masters at their crafts.

25. NOT SCARED OF HEIGHTS?

One of the most famous things to do in Palm Springs is to ride the aerial tramway. The tram is 10 minutes/ 2.5 miles and is the worlds largest rotating tramcar. You'll get to see the natural wilderness of the San Jacinto state park and see the vistas of the valleys. At the top, there's restaurants and observation decks to take in the scenery. There are also numerous hiking trails to take advantage of. This is a must for any traveler and is one of the top things to do, especially if you're coming with your family. Be prepared for the weather to drop at least 10 degrees on the way up.

26. VINTAGE FLEA MARKET

If you're a vintage lover, make sure you plan your trip to Palm Springs the first weekend of the month, from October to May to attend the vintage flea market. Visiting only costs $5 and it runs for 6 hours. Think, Los Angeles Rose Bowl flea market, but on a smaller scale. There are over 40 different vendors bringing an array of midcentury modern furniture, original art pieces, vintage clothing, and collectable China. Some of my favorite booths have 1960's retro baby doll dresses, one of a kind embroidered linen tops, and silk paisley pants. For furniture, you'll find walnut credenzas, bow pin console tables, and cane chairs. Prices are reasonable, but I'd always bargain. You can typically get at least a 10% discount.

At the market, besides furniture and clothing, there are a couple food/desert booths. You can always count on Gelato Grannuci and Chef Tanya's Kitchen to be there. Granucci is one of Palm Springs not so secret best gelato ever. The shop is family owned with their ancestor's gelato recipe from Italy. Chef Tanya's Kitchen is another local favorite featuring vegan food.

27. DRESS FOR ELEGANCE

Melvyn's is more of a time capsule more than anything. Melvyn's is a famous restaurant inside the 30-room boutique hotel name Ingleside Inn. The hotel was fitted by a Spanish colonial revival specialist and coveted Santa Barbara architect, George Smith. With it's lovely antiques that spared no expense, it is a vision and it attracted many of Hollywood's elites including Marilyn Monroe and Elizabeth Taylor in the 40's and 50's. Stays were by invite only and dinner guests needed approval. This was the spot to be in town. Now, it's casual elegance has fully transcended time and Melvyn's remains to be a hot spot for locals and travelers alike.

You can drive your car inside the gate with the valet staff through the U-shaped driveway. Stepping outside, you will be greeted by a plethora of bougainvillea sprawling the grounds. The landscaping is covered in red, yellow, orange blooms and fitted with cactus that surrounds the entrance. The hotels old school charm brings you back to a decade of the past.

28. LIVE MUSIC AND WINE

V lounge is full of midcentury modern vibes in a large airy room with small, sectioned areas which make it easy to come as a group and feel like you're in the privacy of your own home. The wine bar showcases plenty of international wines, craft beers and specialty cocktails. The owner James Mortensen does a great job of playing with color and texture when picking out furniture and wall colors. The best thing about the V is the live music and karaoke. Every Wednesday night is karaoke night where you can belt out your favorite song, Jolene to a crowd of smiling faces. Live music is every Monday, and it features Leanna and Miguel who bring jazz, Latin, and bossa nova to the crowd.

V is a local fan favorite. You will see the same groups of people go to karaoke and live music nights and soon you will know everyone by a first name basis. A month later, when you walk in, you'll hear,

"Hey [FNAME], I have your Dao poured already waiting for you". It's a cozy spot.

29. BEST MARGARITA IN PALM SPRINGS?

The Kimpton has the best margarita in Palm Springs. In addition to the best margarita, they also have the best view to sip on the margarita. The Kimpton Rowan is a new hotel in the heart of downtown a block from Palm Canyon Drive and features a rooftop pool and terrace. The rooftop offers a sophisticated, yet relaxed atmosphere fitted with day beds and cabanas. For those folks who are not staying at the hotel, they can still enjoy a pool day. Kimpton offers daytime and evening cabana rentals with a minimum food and beverage order. This is also a great option for locals on those days over 100 degrees who don't have their own pools. What's a better way to cool off in the summer?

30. VEGAN DELIGHT

One of Palm Springs most well-known restaurants is Chef Tanya's Kitchen. The shop opened in 2017 and first started as a manufacturing facility for tempeh and soon after, it expanded into a takeout deli and a curated marketplace. Tanya's is all vegan. They are known for their mixtures of sauces and the Chupacabra sandwich is a testament. This is one of those places where you taste it once and you're hooked. The most popular dishes are the Cubano which uses seitan instead of chicken, Guadalajara burger which uses tempeh instead of beef, and the Coachella Forever salad, which is embellished with avocado, quinoa, jicama, and toasted pepitas. You can also pick up deli meats from the restaurant, so you'd be able to make your own sandwiches at home. Even if you aren't vegan, this is a special spot to try.

It's always busy at Tanya's so if you can, place an order online and pick it up. If you go without calling in, be prepared to wait for at least 20-30 minutes for your food. It's a hot spot because the food is so good that it attracts vegans and non-vegans alike. There's something about the unique mixture of sauces that has you hooked!

31. OPEN HOUSES

The housing market in Palm Springs is booming! According to redfin, home prices were up 47% compared to last year with the median home price of $668K. Many homes sell within 29 days of being on the market. Right now, it's tough to buy a home because there's so much competition, a lot of that has to do with investors coming in with all cash offers. Despite the craze in the housing market, there are always beautiful open houses on the weekends to check out even if you're not seriously consider buying. Tour some 1930's historic Spanish style triplexes in the Warm Sands neighborhood, or some luxury 2,000+ square foot homes in The Mesa. Get some good design inspiration for free.

32. FEELING IN THE MOOD FOR CABARET?

There's always a party happening at Oscars. Oscars is a restaurant/bar with a massive outdoor entertainment area which is home to one of Palm Springs longest running Sunday drag brunch. They also host weekly events such as Mimosa Men Saturdays and Bitchiest Brunch Sundays. Go for the entertainment and be pleasantly surprised by the food. You might just run into celebrities like Priscilla Presley who made an appearance in January.

33. WELCOME ABOARD PS AIR

Have you ever wondered what it would be like to fly in first class sipping on bubbly? One of the most underrated bars in Palm Springs is PS Air. The bar is in a speakeasy inside a wine bar called Bouschet. You walk inside and you are immediately transported into a plane. The servers are decked in their flight attendant outfits and greet you with a smile while walking you down the flight aisle to your seat. If you arrive at off peak hours, you'll likely find some opening in the first-class section. You feel the air condition blasted high as if you're on a real plane. The entire room is decked out with vintage aviation memorabilia while a historic video of planes flying over plays in the background.

Try the tri tip sliders, sesame chicken skewers, and the tom turkey balls. Best of all, every Sunday is a boozy disco brunch with entertainment staring the PS

Air Fly Girls. There are also special events happening so book early because spots fill up fast. What's better than a disco boozy brunch with a drag show on a mock airplane? This is a Palm Springs best known secret!

34. SUPPORTING MEDICAL HEALTHCARE THROUGH RESALE

DAP Health is an advocacy-based health center in Palm Springs that offers pharmacy, medical and mental healthcare, STI treatments, and dentistry for those who can't afford it. Revivals is a widely popular secondhand store for clothing and furniture. People will donate their secondhand clothing and all the profits are given to DAP. 100% of the proceeds go to the funding. Each year the organization donates over $1 million. Revivals is a long-standing store with multiple locations in the desert community including Rancho Mirage, Palm Desert, and Palm Springs. You never know what treasures you may find there.

The Palm Springs store has arguably, the best goodies. You can find name brand linen tops and dresses, relevant books Oprah Winfrey's book club, and vibrant retro jewelry. Prices are low and there are even additional discounts if you are an active military member, senior, or a student. I was able to furnish my apartment through Revivals at a fraction of what it would be at a retail store.

35. UNASSUMING STRIP MALL

You go to a strip mall and the restaurant name says Bar/Food. This is the type of place that one would overlook but that's the irony and why Paul O'Halloran named it. On any given night be expected to wait to get a seat, unless you show up promptly at 5pm. Inside you'll find plush bar stools, dimly lit lights, and a massive mahogany bar fitted with a plethora of hard alcohol and wine. Paul used to work at Mr. Lyons steakhouse, a famous high-end restaurant. I heard that he took some of the staff from Lyons to Bar/Food, or otherwise called, "Paul Bar". This spot attracts all the people who want good food and drinks but not the fuss that comes with going to a fancy upscale restaurant. You know what you're getting when you go to Paul Bar.

The food is phenomenal. The menu is small, they specialize on a couple fan favorites. You must try the yellow curry and the pork pulled sandwich. Visiting Paul Bar won't break the bank either, entrée dishes are within $15-20 compared to other high-end spots charging at least double to triple.

36. CV LINK BIKE TRAIL

Looking for a bike trail where the path goes on and on for miles? You have 40 miles of pathway on the CV link trail. The trail has been in development since 2011 and it's meant for low-speed vehicles, bike, pedestrians to move along the Whitewater River. On a Saturday morning, you'll see dozens of folks riding from Palm Springs all the way to Coachella Valley. In the future, the route will connect the Desert Springs community and even as far as the Salton Sea.

37. ALBERT FREY HOUSE

Albert Frey is one of the most influential modern architects in the 1900's and has done a lot for the Palm Springs community. He helped design the Palm Springs City Hall and the renown Aerial Tramway. One of his most popular projects, and his long-time residence is the Frey House, which was completed in 1964. The Frey house is built on a hillside and has large spans of glass within a steel frame. He liked the idea that architecture and nature could co-exist, so you'll see massive bouldering rocks inside the home with glass built around it. Visit the Palm Springs art museum website and book tours to check out this architectural gem yourself.

38. MARIACHIS AND AGUACHILES

El Patio is a family run Mexican restaurant that specializes in margaritas, fajitas, and aguchiles located one block off downtown Palm Canyon Road. The food is phenomenal but also the lively atmosphere. Lanterns and large ficus trees surround the vibrant color walls that enclose the outdoor patio. There's a lot of colorful geometric painted patterns, ceramic figurines, and clay wall hangings indicative of Mexico. On most nights, you'll be able to get serenaded by mariachis who walk around the restaurant and sing sweet Spanish romance songs. El Patio is wonderful place to go with family and typically won't have a wait on the weekdays. Weekends are a different story. Go early!

39. BIG BOWL OF PHO

Contrary to popular belief, winter nights in Palm Springs can get a little chilly. Temperatures will hit 50's and for some, that means soup weather. Fuzion Five, located downtown on Palm Canyon Drive is famous for their pho soup. Pho is made from noodles, bean sprouts, bone beef broth, beef, and herbs. Fuzion has their beef sit in the broth for over 48 hours giving it a rich flavor. Many people love their pho and their lemongrass noodles. Locals love this place so much that they voted it best in the valley in 2019. The restaurant itself is no frills, located on the very edge of the strip. You won't find many tourists here.

While there isn't an influx of Asian food in the desert, eating at Fuzion is as authentic as going to a pho restaurant in Vietnam. The food also comes out quick! I like to go get pho after a morning walk through downtown and even then, the tables are filled.

40. PLAYGROUND OF THE STARS

Perched among the mountains are many magical dwellings. These homes are an oasis like no other. A lot of these midcentury modern and Spanish colonial homes were owned by old movie stars. In the 30-50's many celebrities went to Palm Springs to enjoy pool time and to indulge themselves. These architectural gems have become celebrated and are the fabric of the city. One, owned by Leonardo DiCaprio, purchased in 2014 for 5 million, built in 1964, has a historic past. The home was lived in by Dinah Shore, originally built for her. For those who would like to experience to see the property, it's currently listed on short term rental sites for about ~4k/night.

41. SPA DAY

Palm Springs plays on the mind, heart, and senses with a stunning combination of trendy hotels, shopping, and spas. One spa in particular, Spa at the Andreas is known for their high-end luxury services in a relaxing atmosphere. When you go, expect to have one of the best massages of your life, especially if you get Liz. The deep tissue massage feels like a massage you'd get at a chiropractor office. The movements are artfully calculated. You'll receive a harmonious experience that everyone visiting Palm Springs should experience. Andreas also has packages for someone who wants to get facials, massages, and body scrubs. Being there is a slice of heaven!

Many of their daily deals include facial and massage combinations. You can go early and use their facilities, which is all included. Use the dry sauna, or take a dip in their pool, take a quick shower, and get ready for the services.

42. YOU CAN ALWAYS COUNT ON THE ACE HOTEL

When you're in the mood for a music or wellness event, you can count on the Ace Hotel in Palm Springs to have a remedy. The Ace is a popular hotel among millennials due to it's laid-back artsy vibe. You walk in and you are welcomed by a mixture of CDs on display. The CDs include The Strokes, Artic Monkeys, and The Beastie Boys. The staff are all young and quick witted. The hotel itself takes an older 1950's style cabin vibe and is fit with natural elements for furnishings. Think hipster desert retreat with a chill vibe, tons of intimate areas where you can have some privacy. There's also an approachable restaurant which is very popular in the area, Kings Highway. Get the chicken sandwich!

Some other good perks are that the Ace offers sunset yoga under the stars and open air jazz and dinner series. When there's larger events happening in the area, such as the annual music festival, Coachella, Ace will host larger daytime parties. For those who are looking for a festive place to stay, look no further. This is a hot spot among millennials looking for a good vibe.

43. THURSDAYS IN THE DESERT

Every Thursday from 6-10pm Palm Springs hosts "Villagefest" which is a street market that displays 180+ local vendors. Indian canyon drive is transformed into a festive fair. Have your credit cards ready because there's a ton of unique items for anyone in your party. You'll find handmade toe rings and anklets, fresh baked bread and brownies, paintings, handmade almond toffee and more. The fair is always very crowded despite the weather constraints in the summer. I recommend starting the night by getting a gelato at Granucci's and slowly make your way down the street. The fair is dog friendly as well so bring the pooches!

The fair does get packed so if your dog gets skittish or anxious around many people, this isn't the event for them. Some folks bring their dogs in a wheelbarrow or carriage and roll them around. If you go, look out for the great Great Dane dog, Daisy who is there every single Thursday. She's a sweetheart.

44. FRESH PRODUCE

Every Saturday, from October to May from 8:30 to 1:30pm, you'll find the Farmers Market at the Palm Springs cultural center. The farms are certified which pertains to having all the farmers own and operate state certified farms. Some are certified as organic, and all vendors have certificates that guarantee that the produce is grown on their California farms. This is a wonderful place to find fresh agricultural and related products. The farmer's market is free for admission.

45. GO SEE THE WINDMILLS

If you're driving to Palm Springs from Los Angeles, you will notice these massive windmills on the right-hand side. The wind turbines have been gathering attention since 1982 and have become an iconic feature of the area. There are self-driving tours available where you are in your car and guided along with an audio program. In the program, you'll get an introduction to the wind farm and an overview of wind energy with the evolution of wind turbines. The tour will take roughly ~1.5 hours depending on pace.

46. WALK ALONG THE MOVIE COLONY

The neighborhood, The Movie Colony is home to many prestigious homes owned by some of the largest Hollywood stars Dinah Shore and Cary Grant. To this day, many of the homes in Movie Colony are concealed by rows of enormous hedges giving it an understated private appeal. Hands down, it's the neighborhood with the most greenery. You'll see massive hedges that have been around for decades. One of the main attractions is also the Ruth Hardy park, which fills up 22 acres of pristine grass. Dogs and humans love the park alike.

47. TASTE OF DEEP DISH

Are you from Chicago and you miss deep dish? Giuseppe's is the best place in the desert to get gourmet pizza and pasta. The restaurant is nestled at the end of a mall in South Palm Springs with indoor and outdoor dining. As you walk in, the aroma of tomato sauce and fresh bread fills your nostrils. The cannoli, margarita pizza, fried raviolis, shrimp scampi, and antipasto salad are dishes to try. The portions are large so there will be food to take home.

One of the best things about Giuseppe's is their weekend evening happy hour. You can get a personal pizza for $8 and pair it with a salad for $5. Add a cabernet and you are set. Happy hour is only available at the bar, so get there as the night begins around 5pm.

48. DOWNTOWN ART CENTER

The desert art center, established in 1950 is the oldest art organization in the entire Coachella valley. The center is in a 1927 heritage building, which was the first school of Palm Springs. The art center is a special place to find well curated shows of local artists and affordable non-local art. I love this spot because it's run by volunteers and friendly artists and all proceeds support visual arts programming for kids. The center provides affordable art education programs for all ages and holds social events bringing the art community together.

49. HIKE IT OUT

For those who are looking for a more strenuous hike where big horn sheep sightings are common, go hike the South Lykken Trail. The trail is an 8.8 mile out and back trail in Palm Springs, only a couple minutes driving from downtown. The elevation gain is ~2,200 ft and it takes on average 4hr 30min to complete. This isn't going to be a brisk family walk. Go in the morning before it gets well over 100 degrees in the summer. You'll see many morning hikers prepared with their hiking sticks and multiple water bottles. The initial ascent leads to the Smionetta Kenneth vista, which has break taking view of the valley. You'll see colorful and lush vegetation and many diverse species of birds.

50. WHERE DOGS BRING THEIR HUMANS

Have you ever been to a restaurant serving food for dogs? At Boozehounds, you can find a robust dog menu featuring chicken bowls with veggies and hard-boiled eggs as well as chicken broth with doggie biscuit crumbles. Aside from their dog dishes, their human food is fantastic as well. Boozehounds is known for their interior design and their eclectic multifaceted 7,000 square foot space. There's a cabana bar, open air atrium, patio with indoor and outdoor dining. The southern California menu has a hint of Japanese influence with all locally sourced ingredients. On the weekend, you'll find a crowded outdoor patio with King Charles cavaliers, German shepherds, poodle mixes, and many miniature schnauzers. Go for the dogs, stay for the food.

From time to time, Boozehounds also hosts unique events in their space. They team up with local chef de cuisines at popular restaurants, owners of local desert breweries and they create a multi course experiences. These ticketed events are popular and attracts a younger audience around. Over New Years Eve, they had a ticketed celebration showcasing a local house DJ and festive cocktails and a pre- fixed menu. This is an ideal spot to check out for a good time with friends.

TOP REASONS TO BOOK THIS TRIP

Mountains: The San Jacinto mountains are breathtaking. Anywhere you are in Palm Springs, you'll feel that peace of residing close to nature.

History: The architectural beauty is all surrounding. There's something special about walking through Old Las Palmas, The Mesa, and the Historic Tennis club and seeing all the legendary Palm Springs homes by notable architects.

Weather: Palm Springs in the winter has one of the best climates in all the world. Temperatures will hover around low to mid 70 degrees.

DID YOU KNOW?

1.   Did you know that there's a variety of day trips from Palm Springs that are only an hour away?

One of the best national parks, Joshua Tree is conveniently located 1 hour from Palm Springs. The park is famous for it's unique desert landscape and its night photography of the abundance stars.

2.   Why is Palm Springs called Palm Springs?

The early Spanish explorers called the area of what is now known as Palm Springs, "la Palma de la Mano de Dios" which translates to "The Palm of God's Hand". This is thought that the name Palm Springs came from this Spanish phrase.

3.   Did you know that the date gardens in greater Palm Springs produce more than 80% of the dates that supply the entire United States?

The area is known for being the nations date capital.

4.   Did you know that the median home price in Palm Springs shot up ~50% from 2021?

According to redfin.com, the median price is now $750K in Palm Springs. ~5% of prices sell for over asking. Typically, homes sell after ~25 days on the market. Many homes get multiple offers. The surrounding desert cities such as Palm Desert also have a competitive market.

5.   Did you know Palm Springs is growing at a rate of 0.33% annually?

6.   Did you know that the median age of Palm Springs residents is ~55 years old?

Palm Springs is known for being a retirement community where folks come to golf, relax, and enjoy the warm weather.

7.   Did you know Palm Springs played an important role in World War II?

The desert was a training ground for General George S. Patton's troops. This was prior to the North African invasion. One of the famous hotels, El

Mirador, was purchased by the US government and it was turned into a general hospital. Today, this is known as the Desert Regional medical center.

8.　　Did you know one of the neighboring cities of Palm Springs, Desert Hot Springs is home to one of the greatest mineral water aquifers in the world?

You'll be able to experience natural temperatures of up to 180 degrees. The healing oasis has the purest hot and cold mineral springs in the world, due to an underground aquifer beneath the city. Many boutique hotels build on top of these aquifers and market having their own private mineral pools for guests.

9.　　Did you know the BNP Paribas Tennis Tournament is held in the neighboring city of Indian Wells?

Every year, Indian Wells hosts the Indian Wells Masters, known more popularly as BNP Paribas, 25 minutes from Palm Springs. The tournament lasts for two weeks, and it attracts high levels of players from around the world. The stadium features 16,100 seats and is the second largest stadium in the world.

OTHER RESOURCES:

Map of Palm Springs:
https://visitpalmsprings.com/maps/

Palm Springs historic society:
https://pshistoricalsociety.org/

Redfin housing market:
https://www.redfin.com/city/14315/CA/Palm-Springs/housing-market

Palm Springs demographic and growth:
https://worldpopulationreview.com/us-cities/palm-springs-ca-population

Greater Palm Springs:
https://www.visitgreaterpalmsprings.com/coachella-valley/desert-hot-springs/

Indian wells BNP Paribas:
https://www.tours4tennis.com/bnp-paribas-open

PACKING AND PLANNING TIPS

A Week before Leaving

- Arrange for someone to take care of pets and water plants.

- Email and Print important Documents.

- Get Visa and vaccines if needed.

- Check for travel warnings.

- Stop mail and newspaper.

- Notify Credit Card companies where you are going.

- Passports and photo identification is up to date.

- Pay bills.

- Copy important items and download travel Apps.

- Start collecting small bills for tips.

- Have post office hold mail while you are away.

- Check weather for the week.

- Car inspected, oil is changed, and tires have the correct pressure.

- Check airline luggage restrictions.

- Download Apps needed for your trip.

Right Before Leaving

- Contact bank and credit cards to tell them your location.

- Clean out refrigerator.

- Empty garbage cans.

- Lock windows.

- Make sure you have the proper identification with you.

- Bring cash for tips.

- Remember travel documents.

- Lock door behind you.

- Remember wallet.

- Unplug items in house and pack chargers.

- Change your thermostat settings.

- Charge electronics, and prepare camera memory cards.

READ OTHER
GREATER THAN A TOURIST
BOOKS

> TOURIST

Follow us on Instagram for beautiful travel images:
http://Instagram.com/GreaterThanATourist

Follow *Greater Than a Tourist* on Amazon.

CZYKPublishing.com

> TOURIST

At *Greater Than a Tourist*, we love to share travel tips with you. How did we do? What guidance do you have for how we can give you better advice for your next trip? Please send your feedback to CZYKPublishing@gmail.com as we continue to improve the series. We appreciate your constructive feedback. Thank you.

METRIC CONVERSIONS

TEMPERATURE

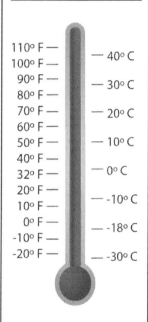

110° F —	— 40° C
100° F —	
90° F —	— 30° C
80° F —	
70° F —	— 20° C
60° F —	
50° F —	— 10° C
40° F —	
32° F —	— 0° C
20° F —	
10° F —	— -10° C
0° F —	— -18° C
-10° F —	
-20° F —	— -30° C

To convert F to C:

Subtract 32, and then multiply by 5/9 or .5555.

To Convert C to F:

Multiply by 1.8
and then add 32.

32F = 0C

LIQUID VOLUME

To Convert:..................Multiply by
U.S. Gallons to Liters............... 3.8
U.S. Liters to Gallons 26
Imperial Gallons to U.S. Gallons 1.2
Imperial Gallons to Liters....... 4.55
Liters to Imperial Gallons 22
1 Liter = .26 U.S. Gallon
1 U.S. Gallon = 3.8 Liters

DISTANCE

To convert ....Multiply by
Inches to Centimeters 2.54
Centimeters to Inches 39
Feet to Meters..................... .3
Meters to Feet 3.28
Yards to Meters 91
Meters to Yards 1.09
Miles to Kilometers 1.61
Kilometers to Miles............ .62
1 Mile = 1.6 km
1 km = .62 Miles

WEIGHT

1 Ounce = .28 Grams
1 Pound = .4555 Kilograms
1 Gram = .04 Ounce
1 Kilogram = 2.2 Pounds

TRAVEL QUESTIONS

- Do you bring presents home to family or friends after a vacation?

- Do you get motion sick?

- Do you have a favorite billboard?

- Do you know what to do if there is a flat tire?

- Do you like a sun roof open?

- Do you like to eat in the car?

- Do you like to wear sun glasses in the car?

- Do you like toppings on your ice cream?

- Do you use public bathrooms?

- Did you bring a cell phone and does it have power?

- Do you have a form of identification with you?

- Have you ever been pulled over by a cop?

- Have you ever given money to a stranger on a road trip?

- Have you ever taken a road trip with animals?

- Have you ever gone on a vacation alone?

- Have you ever run out of gas?

- If you could move to any place in the world, where would it be?

- If you could travel anywhere in the world, where would you travel?

- If you could travel in any vehicle, which one would it be?

- If you had three things to wish for from a magic genie, what would they be?

- If you have a driver's license, how many times did it take you to pass the test?

- What are you the most afraid of on vacation?

- What do you want to get away from the most when you are on vacation?

- What foods smell bad to you?

- What item do you bring on ever trip with you away from home?

- What makes you sleepy?

- What song would you love to hear on the radio when you're cruising on the highway?

- What travel job would you want the least?

- What will you miss most while you are away from home?

- What is something you always wanted to try?

- What is the best road side attraction that you ever saw?

- What is the farthest distance you ever biked?

- What is the farthest distance you ever walked?

- What is the weirdest thing you needed to buy while on vacation?

- What is your favorite candy?

- What is your favorite color car?

- What is your favorite family vacation?

- What is your favorite food?

- What is your favorite gas station drink or food?

- What is your favorite license plate design?

- What is your favorite restaurant?

- What is your favorite smell?

- What is your favorite song?

- What is your favorite sound that nature makes?

- What is your favorite thing to bring home from a vacation?

- What is your favorite vacation with friends?

- What is your favorite way to relax?

- Where is the farthest place you ever traveled in a car?

- Where is the farthest place you ever went North, South, East and West?

- Where is your favorite place in the world?

- Who is your favorite singer?

- Who taught you how to drive?

- Who will you miss the most while you are away?

- Who if the first person you will contact when you get to your destination?

- Who brought you on your first vacation?

- Who likes to travel the most in your life?

- Would you rather be hot or cold?

- Would you rather drive above, below, or at the speed limited?

- Would you rather drive on a highway or a back road?

- Would you rather go on a train or a boat?

- Would you rather go to the beach or the woods?

TRAVEL BUCKET LIST

1.

2.

3.

4.

5.

6.

7.

8.

9.

10.

NOTES

Made in United States
Troutdale, OR
11/02/2024

24383635R00053